Christmas Jokes

Knock, knock . . .
Who's there?
Jane.
Jane who?
Jane who did the
drawings in this book.

(That's Jane Eccles, who loves drawing
and works in a tiny room in her house
in Hampshire, where she lives with her
husband and son and small grey cat.)

Christmas Jokes

Illustrated by Jane Eccles

MACMILLAN CHILDREN'S BOOKS

First published 2013 by Macmillan Children's Books
a division of Macmillan Publishers Limited
20 New Wharf Road, London N1 9RR
Basingstoke and Oxford
Associated companies throughout the world
www.panmacmillan.com

ISBN 978-1-4472-2774-8

Text copyright © Macmillan Children's Books 2013
Illustrations copyright © Jane Eccles 2013

The right of Jane Eccles to be identified as the
illustrator of this work has been asserted by her in accordance
with the Copyright, Designs and Patents Act 1988.

1 3 5 7 9 8 6 4 2

A CIP catalogue record for this book is available from
the British Library.

Printed and bound by CPI Group (UK) Ltd, Croydon CR0 4YY

For Thomas, Miranda,
James, Edie and Elie

CONTENTS

FATHER CHRISTMAS

What's red and white and
goes up and down?
Father Christmas stuck in a lift.

What's red and white,
bounces and goes 'Ho ho ho'?
Father Christmas on a pogo stick.

What did Mrs Christmas say
to Father Christmas?
'It looks like rain, dear.'

What nationality is
Father Christmas?
North Polish.

What's red and white,
red and white, red and white?
Father Christmas rolling down a hill.

How does Father Christmas feel
when he's stuck in a chimney?
Claus-trophobic.

What do you get when Father
Christmas comes down the
chimney and lands in the fire?
Crisp Kringle.

What kind of motorbike does
Father Christmas have?
A Holly-Davidson.

What do you call people who
are afraid of Father Christmas?
Claus-trophobic.

What do you get if you cross
Father Christmas with a duck?
A Christmas quacker.

What says 'Oh oh oh'?
*Father Christmas walking
backwards.*

What does Father Christmas
use when he goes fishing?
His North Pole.

What makes Father Christmas
such a good racing-car driver?
He's always in pole position.

What do you call a
smelly Santa?
Farter Christmas.

Why does Father Christmas come
down the chimney on Christmas Eve?
Because it soots him.

What goes 'Ho ho swoosh',
Ho Ho Swoosh?
Father Christmas in a revolving door.

Why does Father Christmas
have three gardens?
So that he can 'Hoe hoe hoe'.

What do you call Father
Christmas after he has
come down the chimney?
Cinder Claus.

If Santa Claus and Mrs Claus had a
child, what would it be called?
Subordinate Clause.

What is Father
Christmas's favourite pizza?
One that's deep-pan, crisp and even.

What is Father
Christmas's wife called?
Mary Christmas.

What do you get if you
cross Father Christmas
with a detective?
Santa Clues.

Why didn't Father Christmas get wet when he lost his umbrella?
It wasn't raining.

What do you call a man who claps at Christmas?
Santapplause.

Who carries Father Christmas's books for him?
His books-elf.

CHRISTMAS TIME

What happens if you eat the
Christmas decorations?
You get tinsellitis.

Christmas: The time when
everyone gets Santamental.

Why did the turkey join the band?
Because it had the drumsticks.

Why is a Christmas tree
like a bad knitter?
They both drop their needles.

Bob: Why did your dad get splinters from the book you gave him for Christmas?
James: It was a logbook.

What is the best key to get at Christmas?
A tur-key.

Who hides in a bakery at Christmas?
A mince spy.

Doctor: Nurse! I want to operate.
Take this patient to the theatre.
Nurse: Oh good! I love a nice
pantomime at Christmas.

Why is a Christmas
pudding like the sea?
They're both full of currants.

Child: Mum, can I have a
dog for Christmas?
*Mother: No. You can have
turkey like everyone else.*

Who is never hungry at Christmas?
The turkey. He's always stuffed.

What do you get if you cross an
apple with a Christmas tree?
A pineapple.

Why are Christmas trees
always warm?
Because they're fir trees.

Why did the Christmas
cake go to the doctor?
Because it was feeling crummy.

What do sad Christmas trees do?
Pine a lot.

What do you call a letter sent up the
chimney on Christmas Eve?
Black-mail.

What happened to the
turkey at Christmas?
It was gobbled.

Child 1: We had
Grandma for Christmas dinner.
Child 2: Really? We had turkey.

What do vampires put on
their turkey at Christmas?
Grave-y.

Why did the turkey cross the road?
To prove that he wasn't a chicken.

What's the most popular
whine at Christmas?
*'Do I have to eat my
Brussels sprouts?'*

Mother: Eat your Brussels sprouts –
they're good for growing children.
Son: Why would I want to grow children?

What's the best thing to put
in a Christmas cake?
Your teeth.

What does Tarzan sing at
Christmas time?
'Jungle Bells'.

What did the grape say to the raisin?
"Tis the season to be jelly.'

What did the Christmas
stocking say when it
had a hole in it?
'Well, I'll be darned!'

Who brings presents to
baby sharks?
Santa Jaws.

What makes a
Christmas
tree noisy?
Its bark.

What should
you give a deaf
fisherman for Christmas?
A herring aid.

What is the best
Christmas present?
*Difficult to say, but a
drum takes a lot of beating.*

What did one angel say to the other?
'Halo there.'

Dad: Would you like a
pocket calculator for Christmas?
*Son: No thanks. I already
know how many pockets I have.*

Who beats his chest and
swings from Christmas
cake to Christmas cake?
Tarzipan.

What did the big candle
say to the little candle?
'I'm going out tonight.'

Why do mummies like
Christmas so much?
Because of all the wrapping.

Where does mistletoe go to find fame?
Holly-wood.

What did Adam say the
night before Christmas?
'It's Christmas, Eve.'

What kind of paper
likes music?
Wrapping paper.

What happened to the man
who stole an Advent Calendar?
He got twenty-five days.

What's white and goes up?
A confused snowflake.

Lucy: Did you like the dictionary
I gave you for Christmas?
Ben: Yes, I've been trying to find the
words to thank you.

What comes at the end
of Christmas Day?
The letter Y.

What did one Christmas light
say to the other Christmas light?
'You light me up.'

Why is it so cold at Christmas?
Because it's Decembrrrrrrrrr.

Where is the best place to
put your Christmas tree?
*Between your Christmas two
and your Christmas four.*

What time is it when little white flakes
fall past the classroom window?
Snow and tell.

SANTA'S LITTLE HELPERS

Why did the elf curl up in the fireplace?
He wanted to sleep like a log.

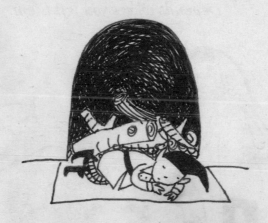

Why was Santa's little
helper depressed?
He had low elf-esteem.

How do elves greet each other?
'*Small world, isn't it?*'

Where do you find elves?
Depends where you left them.

What is the difference between
a biscuit and a reindeer?
You can't dunk a reindeer in your tea.

What is the wettest
animal in the world?
The rain-deer.

If athletes get athlete's foot, what
do Father Christmas's elves get?
Mistle-toes.

Why did the elf wear
sunglasses on the beach?
Because he didn't want to be recognized.

What do elves learn at school?
The elf-abet.

What do reindeer always
say before telling a joke?
'This one will sleigh you.'

What did the elf say when
he was teaching Santa
Claus to use the computer?
'First, yule log in.'

What kind of bread do elves
make sandwiches with?
Shortbread.

What do the reindeer sing to
Father Christmas on his birthday?
'Freeze a jolly good fellow...'

How do elves go upstairs?
In an elf-evator.

How many legs does a reindeer have?
Six. Forelegs at the front and two at the back.

What do you call a stingy elf?
Elf-ish.

What do you call a
reindeer with no eyes?
No idea.

What do you call a reindeer
with no eyes and no legs?
Still no idea.

What do you call a reindeer with
a number plate on its rump?
Reg.

How do you make a slow reindeer fast?
Don't feed him.

Why don't reindeer like penguins?
They can't get the wrappers off.

What do reindeer have
that no other animals do?
Baby reindeer.

How do you describe an elf
who refuses to have a shower?
Elf-ully smelly.

How many elves does it take
to change a light bulb?
*Ten. One to change the light bulb
and nine to stand under him
on each other's shoulders.*

Why are reindeer
such bad dancers?
They have two left feet.

Which of Father Christmas's reindeer
needs to mind his manners?
Rude-olph.

Why did the elves spell
Christmas N-O-E?
Because Santa had said,
'No L.'

What would you call an elf
who has just won the lottery?
Welfy.

Why did the reindeer
wear black boots?
*Because his brown ones
were all muddy.*

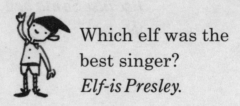

Which elf was the
best singer?
Elf-is Presley.

Why do reindeer wear fur coats?
Because they'd look silly in polyester.

What do they call a
wild elf in Texas?
Gnome on the range.

What do you call a reindeer
in the Sahara desert?
Lost.

If a reindeer lost his tail,
where would it go for a new one?
A re-tail store.

Why did the reindeer
cross the road?
Because he was tied to a chicken.

What do you call a reindeer
wearing earmuffs?
Anything you like. He can't hear you.

AT THE NORTH POLE

What often falls at the
North Pole but never gets hurt?
Snow.

What do snowmen
eat for lunch?
Icebergers.

What do you get if you
cross a shark with a snowman?
Frostbite.

What do snowmen eat for breakfast?
Snowflakes.

What's an ig?
*An eskimo's home
without a loo.*

What did one snowman say
to the other snowman?
'Can you smell carrots?'

What goes, 'Now you see me,
now you don't; now you see
me, now you don't.'?
A snowman on a zebra crossing.

Where do polar bears go to vote?
At the North Poll.

What is a snowman's
favourite mode of transport?
An ice-icle.

What do Eskimos use to
hold their houses together?
Ig-glue.

What happens when a
snowman has dandruff?
Snowflakes.

What did the policeman say to the
snowman when he caught him stealing?
'Freeze!'

What do you call a
snowman on rollerskates?
A snow mobile.

How do snowmen greet each other?
'It's ice to meet you.'

What do you call a
snowman in the summer?
A puddle.

What sort of ball doesn't bounce?
A snowball.

What do snowmen
call their money?
Ice lolly.

What does an angry
snowman give you?
The cold shoulder.

What does Frosty the
Snowman drink?
Iced tea.

What does a snowman
take when he gets ill?
A chill pill.

What is a snowman's
favourite Mexican food?
Brrr-itos.

What is white, lives in the North Pole
and runs around naked?
A polar bare.

What does Frosty the
Snowman wear on his head?
An ice cap.

How can you tell a snowman
from a snow-woman?
*The snow-woman is the one
wearing the make-up.*

What do you get when you cross a
snowman with a baker?
Frosty the Dough-man.

Where do snowmen dance?
At snow balls.

What's the difference between
an iceberg and a clothes brush?
*One crushes boats and the other
brushes coats.*

How do you know
when there is a
snowman in your bed?
You wake up wet.

CHRISTMAS BOOK TITLES

The Art of Kissing
Miss L. Toe

Winning at Charades
Vic Tree

Guessing Your Presents
P. King

I'd Rather Have Fish
for Christmas Dinner
Ann Chovie

Too Much Christmas Dinner
O. Beese

How to Get a Great Present
B. Good

101 Cures for Indigestion
Ivor Pain

Sledging for
Beginners
I. C. Bottom

Christmas Questions
I. Dunnoe & Noah Little

Make Your Parents
Get What You Want
Ruth Lesschild

Surprise Present!
Omar Ghosh

What Do You Do After Christmas Dinner?
Clare Inup

Bad Gifts
M. T. Box

CHRISTMAS CRITTERS

What squeaks and is scary?
The Ghost of Christ-mouse Past.

What do angry mice send each other?
Cross-mouse cards.

What do you call
a cat on a beach
at Christmas?
Sandy Claws.

Who delivers Christmas presents to pets?
Santa Paws.

What's green, covered in
tinsel and goes ribbet ribbet?
A mistle-toad.

What is a skunk's favourite
Christmas song?
'Jingle Smells'.

What do you get when you
cross a skunk with a bell?
Jingle smells.

How do sheep greet
each other at Christmas?
A Merry Christmas to ewe.

What do you call a gigantic polar bear?
Nothing, you just run away.

What kind of bird
can write?
A pen-guin.

What's white, furry and
smells of mint?
A polo bear.

What do you call a
lobster who won't share his
Christmas presents?
Shellfish.

What Christmas carol is
popular in the desert?
'O Camel Ye Faithful'.

What kind of pine has
the sharpest needles?
A porcupine.

Why don't penguins fly?
Because they're too short to be pilots.

What's the most
tedious animal?
A polar bore.

What did Santa get
when he crossed a
woodpecker with a tissue?
Rapping paper.

What did the sheep say to the shepherd?
Season's bleatings.

What do
hedgehogs eat for
Christmas dinner?
Prickled onions.

Why do birds fly south in the winter?
Because it's too far to walk.

What is twenty feet tall, has
sharp teeth and goes 'Ho ho ho'?
Tyranno-santa rex.

What do wild animals
sing at Christmas time?
'Jungle bells, jungle bells,
jungle all the way.'

Where do ghosts go
for a Christmas treat?
The phantomime.

Who gives Christmas
presents to chickens?
Santa Clucks.

What sort of insects
love snow?
Mo-ski-toes.

How do you call an Eskimo cow?
An Eskimoo.

What do elephants
sing at Christmas?
'No-elephants, no-elephants.'

Why did Scrooge have a pet lamb?
So that it could say 'baaaaaaa humbug'.

How do cows greet each
other at Christmas?
Merry Chrismoooo.

KNOCK, KNOCK

Knock, knock
Who's there?
Hannah.
Hannah who?
Hannah partridge in a pear tree.

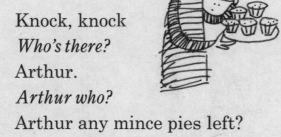

Knock, knock
Who's there?
Arthur.
Arthur who?
Arthur any mince pies left?

Knock, knock
Who's there?
Wenceslas.
Wenceslas who?
Wenceslas train home?

Knock, knock
Who's there?
Carol singers.
*Carol singers! Do you know what flaming
time of night it is?*
No, but if you hum it we'll sing it.

Knock, knock
Who's there?
Snow.
Snow who?
Snow use, I've forgotten my key.

Knock, knock
Who's there?
Jimmy.
Jimmy who?
Jimmy a kiss under the mistletoe.

Knock, knock
Who's there?
Oakham.
Oakham who?
Oakham All Ye Faithful.

Knock, knock
Who's there?
Snow.
Snow who?
Snow business like show business.

Knock, knock
Who's there?
Holly.
Holly who?
Holly-days are here again.

Knock, knock
Who's there?
Our Wayne.
Our Wayne who?
Our Wayne in a manger.

Knock, knock
Who's there?
Doughnut.
Doughnut who?
Doughnut open till Christmas.

Knock, knock
Who's there?
Avery.
Avery who?
Avery Merry Christmas.

Knock, knock
Who's there?
Rabbit.
Rabbit who?
Rabbit up neatly, it's a present.

Knock, knock
Who's there?
Mary.
Mary who?
Mary Christmas.

Knock, knock
Who's there?
Police!
Police who?
Police don't make me eat
Brussels sprouts this year.

Knock, knock
Who's there?
Wanda.
Wanda who?
Wanda know what you're
getting for Christmas?

Knock, knock
Who's there?
Elf.
Elf who?
Elf me wrap this present for Santa.

Knock, knock
Who's there?
Yule.
Yule who?
Yule be sorry if you don't
holly up and elf me wrap
this present for Santa.

DOCTOR, DOCTOR!

Doctor, Doctor, I keep thinking
I'm a Christmas bell.
*Just take these pills and, if they don't
work, give me a ring.*

Doctor, Doctor, Father Christmas
gives us oranges every year and now
I think I'm turning into an orange.
Well that's a juicy story.

Doctor, Doctor, Father Christmas gives
us oranges every year and now I think
I'm turning into an orange.
Have you tried playing squash?

Doctor, Doctor, with all the excitement of Christmas I can't sleep.
Try lying on the edge of your bed ... you'll soon drop off.

Father Christmas: Doctor, Doctor, I feel so unfit.
You need to go to an elf farm.

Doctor, Doctor, I'm scared
of Father Christmas.
*I think you're suffering from
Claus-trophobia.*

Doctor, Doctor, my problem is that
I keep stealing things when I go
Christmas shopping. Can you give
me something for it?
*Try this medicine ... and if it doesn't
work come back and bring me a new video
camera.*

Doctor, Doctor, how do I become
an organ donor before Christmas?
It's easy! Just drop off a piano at my
house tomorrow.

Doctor, Doctor, I think the world
is going to end at Christmas.
Well, I think you should just
enjoy the present.

THE
TRUTH
ABOUT
CHRISTMAS
PHILIP
ARDAGH

HAVE YOU EVER WONDERED?

Who decided to celebrate Christ's birthday on 25 December?

Why we kiss under the mistletoe?

Where the flying reindeer came from?

When the first Christmas card was sent?

What on earth a yule log has to do with Christmas?

What all that holly and ivy is for?

Why Christmas pudding is Christmas-pudding shaped?

★

The answers to these and many other festive questions are
packed within the covers of this gorgeous book.